W9-AAT-382

By Jennifer Guess McKerley

KIDHAVEN PRESS
An imprint of Thomson Gale, a part of The Thomson Corporation

Detroit • New York • San Francisco • New Haven, Conn. • Waterville, Maine • London

For more information, contact
KidHaven Press
27500 Drake Rd.
Farmington Hills, MI 48331-3535
Or you can visit our Internet site at http://www.gale.com

LIBRARY OF CONGRESS CATALOGING-IN-PUBLICATION DATA

McKerley, Jennifer Guess.
The kraken / by Jennifer Mckerley.
p. cm. -- (Monsters)
Includes bibliographical references and index.
ISBN 978-0-7377-3531-4 (hardcover)
1. Sea monsters--North Atlantic Region--Juvenile literature. 2. Giant squids--North Atlantic Region--Juvenile literature. I. Title.
GR910.M37 2008
398.24'54--dc22

2007021294

ISBN-10: 0-7377-3531-7
Printed in the United States of America

Legendary Sea Monster

As a ship sails off the coast of South America, the sailors spy a little island. Although the crew has sailed that part of the sea often, they have never seen this piece of land before. The vessel sails closer. Suddenly the island comes alive. A dark mound rises higher and higher until a terrifying sight appears. A giant sea monster–a kraken–towers over the ship. Its massive eyes glare. Huge tentacles thrash about and surround the vessel. Then one tentacle plucks a man off the deck. The victim screams in horror, but no one can save him as he disappears into the kraken's mouth. Finally the beast plunges back into the sea. Still all is not well. The monster's dive creates a whirlpool.

Like a bug swirling down a drain, the sailors on the ship are sucked under to their deaths.

During the 1600s, sailors in Europe and the Americas told this legend of the kraken, a sea monster of **gargantuan** size. The beast became known as one of most horrifying ocean creatures ever. The earliest stories came from the ancient mythology of Greece and Scandinavia. In Greek tales, a fierce krakenlike beast called Scylla lived on rocks along a narrow channel of water. It had six long necks with dog heads, rows of sharp teeth, twelve legs, and a fish tail. Scylla snatched sailors from passing ships and ate them alive. In Norway and Iceland, popular tales warned of a creature named hafgufa, a hideous sea monster that attacked ships.

All over the world, tales spread about huge octopus-like beasts with long thrashing arms, able to grab the largest warship and drag it into the murky depths of the ocean. The monsters were sometimes called sea serpents and were sometimes said to have fins like a fish. The name "kraken" is Norwegian, meaning an abnormal animal or something twisted.

Terror from the Deep

A book written in 1555 tells of a strange, unusual beast that lived off the coast of Norway. Olaus Mag-

Next page: A Greek ship passes through a narrow channel near the Scylla, a kraken-like beast.

nus, Catholic archbishop of Sweden, studied tales of sea monsters. He reported that seamen had spotted a creature that looked like a tree pulled up by its roots. Sailors estimated that it was 200 feet (61m) long and 20 feet (6m) wide. Magnus described its skin as a dark color that changed quickly, especially when it was frightened. It had eight feet in all with the four biggest ones in the middle. He said its square head bore huge, fiery eyes and prickles that stuck out. A pipe also jutted from its back.

In 1741 minister Hans Egede wrote *The Old Greenland's New Survey*. In it, he describes what he saw on a voyage along the western coast of the island.

> The Monster was of so huge a size, that

"The Sea of Darkness" is a woodcut of a sea snake by Olaus Magnus.

> coming up out of the Water its Head reached as high as the Mast-Head; its Body was as bulky as the Ship, and three or four times as long. It had a long pointed Snout, and spouted like Whale-Fish; great broad Paws, and the Body seemed covered with shell-work, its skin very rugged and uneven. The under Part of its Body was shaped like an enormous huge Serpent, and when it dived under Water, it plunged backwards in the Sea and so raised its Tail aloft, which seemed a whole Ship's Length distant from the bulkiest part of its Body.[1]

Even more amazing claims of size came in the later 1700s. Like many religious leaders, Bishop Erik Pontoppidan of Norway studied and wrote about history and biology. Based on fishermen's accounts, he reported that krakens could be 1.5 miles (2.4km) in circumference, or around, at the broadest part of their bodies. Pontoppidan believed the sea monsters were real. He said a kraken was the most incredible animal in creation. He described its body as round and gray and full of arms or branches. He said it resembled a small island surrounded by floating parts that moved like seaweed. The beast had blue eyes as large as pewter plates and several horns that were thick at the base. Pontoppidan claimed the creature lived at the bottom of the sea and only

came up to feast every three months during calm weather.

Fact or Fiction?

Pierre Dénys de Montfort was a French biologist who also believed the ocean monster existed. In 1802 he wrote a book of stories whalers told about great battles between whales and giant sea beasts. Whalers had long reported that dying whales vomited up squid arms or tentacles, big enough that the animals they belonged to had to be very large. Dénys de Montfort read a report from 1783 about a 26-foot-long (8m) tentacle found in the mouth of a sperm whale. He concluded that giant squid and giant octopi were real and that either could be the legendary sea beast known as the kraken. At that time, the only kind of squid known to exist was no more than 6 inches (15cm) long. People called Dénys de Montfort's book an outlandish fairy tale. Penniless and disgraced, Dénys de Montfort died before he could prove his theory.

In 1857 a Danish biologist, Japetus Steenstrup, examined parts of a dead sea creature and insisted there was indeed a species of giant squid. He named it *Architeuthis dux* (Ark-i-tooth-iss). Like Dénys de Montfort, Steenstrup said it could be the kraken. Still, most educated people and scientists were not convinced. Whether a monster the size of a kraken truly roamed the seas or not, frightening tales continued to be reported.

Pierre Dénys de Montfort believed that the kraken was either a giant squid or octopus (shown here).

In 1873 Theophilus Piccot and his twelve-year-old son, Tom, battled a sea beast off the shore of Newfoundland, Canada. When the creature reared up, it revealed a parrotlike beak the size of a six-gallon barrel. Repeatedly, the monster struck the small boat with its beak while Piccot and his son hit it with oars. Then the creature reached into the boat with two arms that seemed longer than the others. The arms gripped the vessel and yanked it down. Quickly the Piccots grabbed axes. They hacked at the beast's tentacles and severed one about 10 feet (3m) from the animal's head.

Finally the creature swam away. As it did, it released a dark inky substance. Theophilus Piccot estimated the length of the kraken to be 50 to 60 feet (15 to 16m). The piece of tentacle left in the boat measured 19 feet (5.8m) long. He turned the tentacle over to Moses Harvey, a minister, writer, and lecturer in Newfoundland. Harvey was thrilled to receive the amazing limb and immediately had it photographed to prove its existence. He wrote that he had received one of the rarest curiosities in the animal world, an arm of the devil fish, the very creature many biologists said did not exist.

Later in 1873 Harvey received an even greater prize. Fishermen found a giant squid trapped in their net and saved the head and arms. Harvey draped the squid head and tentacles over a tub in his home. Day after day, crowds came to see it. The tentacles measured 24 feet (7m) long, and the

entire animal was 32 feet (9.7m) long. P. T. Barnum, the famous circus and museum owner who bought oddities for his sideshow, tried to buy the squid parts from Harvey.

Instead of selling it, Harvey sent the **specimen** to Dr. Addison Verrill of Yale University. The professor studied squid that were found dead or that died after becoming beached. Two years earlier in 1871, Verrill had received numerous samples. That year, many dead squid were found washed up on shores around the world, especially those of Newfoundland. The cause of the sudden increase in dead squid bodies was not known, but the incidents gave scientists a chance to examine the animals.

By 1881 Verrill had studied 23 giant squid bodies. He wrote scientific articles about the species and helped design the first squid model for a museum. At last, enough evidence had been collected to prove the existence of Dénys de Montfort's monster, the giant squid.

Legendary Monster Explained

Modern experts agree that stories of the legendary kraken probably came from encounters with giant squid or colossal squid. The monster was sometimes described as a giant octopus, but scientists say that squid are more aggressive and more likely to surface. Even though many kraken tales exaggerated the size and strength of the animals, giant squid are of monstrous proportions. The average size of

A giant squid is examined in Australia. It is now believed that stories regarding krakens were really referring to giant squids.

the species is 19.7 to 42.7 feet (6 to 13m), but giant squid can grow as long as 59 feet (18m) and weigh 1 ton (.9MT). Scholars have compared descriptions from ancient sightings with what they know about giant squid, the world's largest mollusk.

The sea beast was said to have a soft body, and mollusks have no backbone. Krakens had eyes as big as dinner plates, and a giant squid has the largest eyes of any animal, as wide as 15 inches (6cm) across. The monster bore many arms, some much

The body of a dead sperm whale shows scores believed to have been caused by fights with giant squids.

longer than others, that reached far. A giant squid has eight arms and two tentacles, which are so long they make up two-thirds of its entire body length. The tentacles can also stretch like rubber bands. Old stories told of the kraken's ability to seize rapidly and grip tightly. A squid's tentacles shoot out like harpoons, grasp, and wrap around the victim. People have even seen severed tentacles that still held on to a boat deck or that closed around a shoe that touched them.

Seamen also witnessed battles between the sea monsters and whales. It is now known that giant squid are a sperm whale's favorite meal, and squid are well equipped to fight. With a row of small suckers, a squid can zip together its two tentacles to form a long club with a clawlike tip. Also, the suckers on the tentacles are lined with sharp teeth. Captured whales often bear round scars the size of squid suckers, which are 1 to 2 inches (2 to 5cm) in diameter. When attacking a ship, a kraken was said to hit the vessel with its mouth, which looked like a parrot's beak–a perfect description of a squid's mouth. A squid's beak can be as wide as 6 inches (15cm) and is strong enough to snap wooden oars in two.

Seamen claimed that krakens gave off an inky substance, and a giant squid has a small ink sac. Stories told of dark sea beasts that could change colors. Giant squid have a thick set of cells called chromatophores. When tightened, the cells produce color changes from pale gray to deep purple. Legends told of a pipe on the back of a kraken or described a whale-fish that spewed water. A squid uses jet propulsion to swim. It sucks in water through its body and expels it through a funnel, a short tubelike opening that sticks out behind its head.

When sketches of a giant squid in water are compared with drawings of krakens from long ago, it is easy to see how people thought they saw a sea

serpent. A tentacle stretched across the ocean's surface could look like a rippling snake. A squid's tail stuck straight up out of water might look like the head of a serpent or monster. Yet by 1881, scientists realized the giant squid existed, and they had enough information to compare it to the legendary kraken and to explain one of the greatest mysteries of the sea.

Chapter 2

The Kraken Lives

For the first time educated people accepted tales about krakens as true and that the monster was actually the giant squid. Finally they believed the stories told over many centuries by uneducated sailors, fishermen, and whalers. Experts took a serious look at old reports and legends to learn from men of the sea and their menacing encounters with the kraken.

In his writings, Bishop Erik Pontoppidan explained that fishermen often **plumbed** the waters to find the monster's location. When their measurements showed the depth of water was shallower than they knew the area to be, it meant a kraken lurked below. It also indicated that the monster was slowly rising from the ocean floor. As it rose to the surface, the animal supposedly pushed large schools of fish up with it. As a result, fisher-

men pulled in a great haul. When they returned to shore with their boats overflowing, other fishermen would say, "you must have fished on kraken." Yet fishing over the creature was said to be a deadly gamble. Pontoppidan wrote that once the monster had risen to twelve **fathoms**, fishermen knew they must quickly get out of the way. Soon the kraken would burst forth like a floating island. It would spew water from its terrible nostrils. Those who fished too long risked getting caught on the back of the rising beast.

A kraken attacks a ship by wrapping its long tentacles around the hull. The beast would eventually pull the vessel below the sea's surface.

The creature did not always attack. Sometimes it merely appeared. Still, nearby ships were in danger. As the creature plunged back into the deep, it created an enormous whirlpool and dangerous waves for many miles. Vessels that never returned home were said to be victims of a kraken.

In the early 1800s, a kraken attacked a ship off the coast of western Africa. Earlier during calm waters, some crew members had been lowered on rigging to clean the bottom parts of the craft. Suddenly a kraken struck. The monster grabbed two men. It tried to snatch another, but the crew hacked at its tentacles until the beast released the man. In an attempt to save the men still in its grasp, sailors speared the creature with five harpoons. Yet the beast snapped the harpoons in half and plummeted below with its victims. The captain claimed the monster never exposed its head. It merely reached up with its long arms. A section of tentacle left behind measured 25 feet (7.6m) long.

English captain Peter M'Quhae (1848) and his crew encountered an enormous creature near the **Cape of Good Hope**. M'Quhae called it a sea serpent, but he said it did not **undulate** like a snake. Instead, it propelled itself through the water.

Opposite: A nineteenth-century illustration shows a French warship trying to capture what it believed to be a kraken. They only ended up capturing the creature's tail.

MESNEL

The beast was at least 60 feet (18m) long and had seaweed-type limbs at its back. The *Illustrated London News* published M'Quhae's report along with drawings based on the crew's descriptions of the animal.

A prominent biologist ridiculed M'Quhae and his crew's sighting. He claimed they were ignorant of zoology. He laughed at their report. M'Quhae and his men all imagined something fantastic, he insisted, or they merely saw a gigantic seal. He said more proof existed for ghosts than for krakens. Still, M'Quhae defended himself and his men. He replied firmly that the creature was no **optical illusion**.

In the North Atlantic Ocean in 1861, a French warship came upon a monstrous kraken in its path. The gigantic animal had huge eyes that gleamed eerily. Its parrotlike beak was surrounded by eight arms between 5 and 6 feet (1.5 to 1.8m) long. The slimy red body extended 18 feet (5.4m). The crew shot at the creature. It dove beneath the surface, but again and again it resurfaced. For three hours, the men and the beast fought. Finally the kraken vomited blood and foam and released a strong odor. The crew caught the injured animal with a rope, which sliced it in two. They only managed to keep a 40-pound (18kg) portion of the tail. When professors at the French Academy of Sciences heard the story, they concluded that the sailors had been victims of mass **hallucination**.

Twenty years later, however, scientists believed their account and older reports as well. Now that experts knew the giant squid existed, they sought to discover more about the creature reported to live at the bottom of the ocean.

Life in the Deep

During the 20th century, scientists learned much about the giant squid. Yet until the 21st century, no one had seen a living giant squid in its deep-sea environment. Teams of scientists began underwater observations in the late 1980s. They attached cameras to the

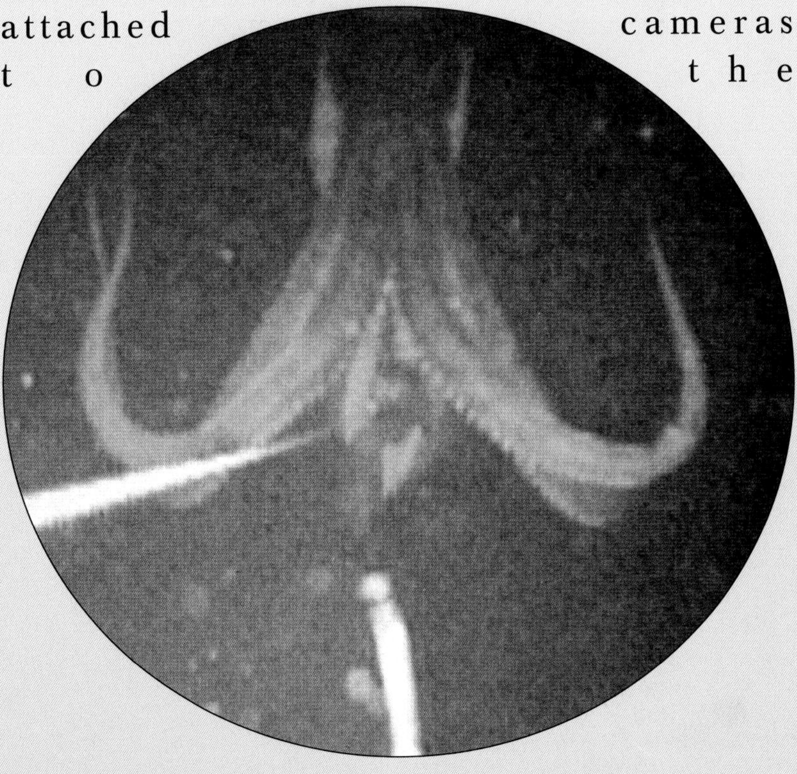

This is one of the first photographs of a giant squid attacking bait in its natural habitat.

backs of sperm whales. They hoped as the whales hunted, the camera would capture a giant squid on film. They were unsuccessful until 2004 when a team of Japanese scientists managed to take the first photos of a giant squid in action.

A team from the National Science Museum of Japan sailed a 5-ton (4.5MT) fishing boat to the ocean area south of Tokyo, where scientists knew whales hunted squid. Crew members dropped a 3,000-foot (914m) line to a depth of 2,950 feet (899m). The line was baited with squid and shrimp. It also held a camera with a flash. Finally after many drops, the squid coiled its arms around the bait like a python wraps its victim. One tentacle became caught in the line. While the squid fought for more than four hours to escape, cameras snapped at least 500 photos–the first ever of a live giant squid in its natural **habitat**. When the squid broke free, it left behind an 18-foot (5.5m) piece of tentacle. Later **DNA** tests confirmed the animal was a giant squid. The crew estimated it had a 7 foot-long (2m) body and a total length of 26 feet (7.9m).

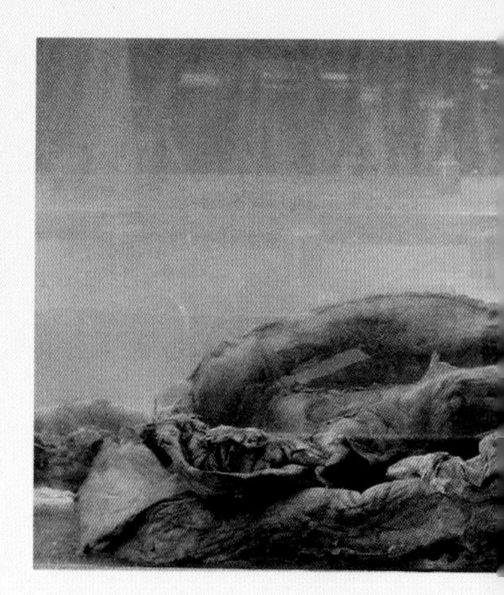

Scientists continue to learn about these fascinating creatures from underwater studies. They also gain new information about giant squid from reports of recent encounters.

Modern Kraken Appearances

In 2003 French yachtsman Olivier De Kersauson and his crew came upon a giant squid in the Atlantic Ocean near Portugal. They saw a tentacle, thicker than a man's leg, stretched across a porthole of the ship. A giant squid had clamped onto the hull of the boat and wrapped its tentacles around the rudder. The animal yanked hard at the vessel, but it released its grip when the ship stopped. De Kersauson said the squid must have been 22 to 26 feet (7 to 8m) long.

In 2006 a fishing boat captured a live giant squid, 28 feet (8.62m) long, off the coast of the **Falkland Islands**. Most giant squid found on beaches or in the stomachs of sperm whales are in bad condition. The capture of a living, whole giant squid is rare. The specimen was sent to the Natural

A giant squid was captured in 2006 and is currently on display at the Natural History Museum in London.

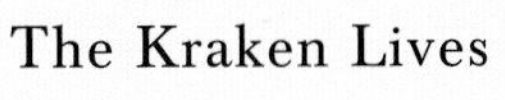

History Museum in London. The terrifying animal, once called the kraken, now lies in a 30-foot (9m) glass tank at the Darwin Centre.

Regularly a few dead or dying squid appear on beaches around the world. The dying creatures do not pose a threat to humans and have provided much knowledge. Sometimes many dying squid turn up at the same time on shores all over the Earth. Just as in the 1870s, numerous dead squid were found on beaches in the 1960s. Scientists can only speculate why the **phenomenon** happens. They think that underwater conditions or diseases that cycle around again after a long period may be the reason. It has been said these conditions return every 90 years. If so, the next appearance of many giant squid on shores should be about 2050.

Scientists believe that squid also surface when they need to mate or search higher waters for food. They do not typically attack people unless they feel threatened. Some stories, however, show that on rare occasions squid will aggressively go after humans. In the 1930s, a giant squid swam awhile beside the *Brunswick*, an oil freighter. Then suddenly it attacked. The squid tried to wrap its arms around the vessel, but it could not grasp the metal of the ship firmly enough. It slipped into the propellers and died.

In 1941 just before World War II, German torpedoes sank the British ship *Britannia* in the Atlantic Ocean. Twelve survivors escaped in a raft. The craft

was too small for all of them so the sailors took turns hanging onto its sides. One night while the raft floated in calm waters, a giant squid reached up and snatched one of the men. The others had no chance to save him. Soon one of the remaining sailors realized something had wrapped around his leg. Lieutenant Cox felt a searing pain as the teeth of the suction cups bit into his skin. With all his strength, he held onto the raft. Finally the squid let go, but its suckers left big round scars on Cox's leg.

Most evidence shows that giant squid avoid humans rather than prey on them. Still, it is the frightening legends that fascinate people and inspire the scary tales of literature and movies.

Forever Famous

Through the ages, countless stories about the sea beasts known as krakens have been told and retold. Alfred Tennyson continued the legend when he wrote *The Kraken* in 1830. Yet he also changed the legend and inspired writers of the next century.

> Below the thunders of the upper deep;
> Far far beneath in the abysmal sea,
> His ancient, dreamless, uninvaded sleep
> The Kraken sleepeth: . . .
>
> There hath he lain for ages, and will lie
> Battening upon huge seaworms in his sleep,
> Until the latter fire shall heat the deep;

Then once by man and angels to be seen,
In roaring he shall rise and on the surface
die.[2]

After Tennyson's poem became well-known, people no longer spoke or wrote about "a kraken." From then on, they said "the Kraken." They named the sea monster as a single fantastic creature instead of one of a species.

The Legend in Literature

It is believed Tennyson's poem inspired Jules Verne when he wrote about the deep home of the giant squid in his book, *Twenty Thousand Leagues Under the Sea*, published in 1870. There are many mentions of the Kraken. The novel is about the fictional Captain Nemo and his submarine, the *Nautilus*. Another novel, the great classic *MobyDick* by Herman Melville (1851), describes a

Alfred Tennyson's poem, The Kraken, *changed the legend of the beast and inspired writers of the next century.*

A scene from Harry Potter and the Chamber of Secrets. *A giant squid lives in the lake next to Hogwarts, the school that Harry Potter attends.*

whaling vessel's encounter with a giant or a colossal squid.

It is thought that Tennyson's poem was also the basis for *The Kraken Wakes* by John Wyndham. In the 1953 science-fiction novel, the Kraken is the cause of a worldwide disaster. Although the Kraken in the story is really a group of aliens from the sea, the invaders seem to be based on the legendary Kraken, and Tennyson's poem is quoted in the book.

In J. R. R. Tolkien's *Lord of the Rings: The Fellowship of the Ring* (1954), the Fellowship battles the Watcher in the Water. It is a multiarmed beast that prowls the waters of Middle-earth. Even though the description of the Watcher is not detailed and it swims in freshwater, the monster is portrayed as krakenlike in the 2001 film based on the book.

The Kraken has turned up in recent books. In the modern Harry Potter series by J. K. Rowling (first published in 1996), a giant squid lives in the lake by Hogwarts, the school of magical arts. Tamora Pierce's *Wild Magic* (1997) tells the story of Daine, a thirteen-year-old who has the amazing ability to communicate with animals. While involved in the problems of a war, she battles griffins, dragons, and the Kraken. Don C. Reed's 1997 novel, *The Kraken*, recounts the tale of Tom Piccot, son of Theophilus, who in real life gave a chopped-off tentacle to Moses Harvey. Based somewhat on the true account, the story relates the bravery of Tommy against the fierce and gigantic Kraken. Five teenagers and an alien **shape shift** into giant squid in the Animorphs book series by K. A. Applegate (1996), which is also a TV series. The characters use their abilities to morph to stop the takeover of Earth by bloodsucking aliens called Yeerks. In *The Secret Life of Owen Skye* by Alan Cumyn (2005), Owen and his brothers have weird adventures that involve an evil giant squid.

TV and Movies

The Kraken also endures as a popular theme for movies and TV shows. The Jules Verne ocean adventure, *Twenty Thousand Leagues Under the Sea*, was made into a movie by Walt Disney in 1954. It features a giant squid attack. Biology professor Aronnax (played by Paul Lukas), his assistant Conseil (Peter Lorre), and a professional whaler, heroic Ned Land (Kirk Douglas), investigate the disappearance of many ships. Although the team suspects the legendary sea creature is responsible, they discover the monster is really a submarine run by Captain Nemo (James Mason).

A team of men encounter a giant squid in the Walt Disney film, Twenty Thousand Leagues Under the Sea.

In the 1981 film *Clash of the Titans*, Princess Andromeda (played by Judi Bowker) is bound to a rock and offered to the Kraken. Perseus (Harry Hamlin) saves her when he cuts off Medusa's head and uses it to turn the Kraken into stone.

In *The Beast*, a 1996 novel by Peter Benchley and also a movie, disturbing events happen at the coast of Graves Point. The only clue to a young couple's disappearance at sea is a large claw stuck in their raft. Marine biologist Dr. Talley (played by Ronald Guttman) decides a gigantic squid or octopus is on the prowl.

A kraken appears in the Disney movie, *Pirates of the Caribbean: Dead Man's Chest* (2006). The beast looks somewhat like a misshapen squid and has a huge mouth lined with six rows of spiked teeth. With its two mighty forearms, it rips apart vessels in seconds and probes about with its suckers to search for humans. One character says it has giant tentacles that will suck a man's face right off and breath that reeks like a thousand rotting carcasses. The Kraken belongs to the heartless Captain Davy Jones (played by Bill Nighy), who has a head like an octopus. Jones summons the beast from the ocean floor to attack his enemies, especially pirate Captain Jack Sparrow (Johnny Depp). Sparrow must battle Jones and his pet kraken in order to seize the magical Dead Man's Chest. If he fails, he will be cursed to serve Captain Jones for eternity.

A kraken appears in the Disney film, Pirates of the Caribbean: Dead Man's Chest. *Captain Davy Jones uses the kraken to attack his enemies.*

In the 2005 Nickelodeon cartoon *Catscratch*, the cat Gordon defeats a red kraken in a battle to earn a new tail. In the *Yu-Gi-Oh!* TV series, there are duel monsters named Fiend Kraken and Fire Kraken. The Kraken in the TV series *Ben 10* is a massive creature that lives in a lake and stays ready to defend it and her giant eggs (2006).

Fun and Games with the Kraken

Books, movies, and television shows have established the fame of the Kraken in modern popular culture. As a result, collectible toy sets and a variety of games present the creature as a star character.

In the original Monster in My Pocket toy series, the Kraken figure was one of the rarest and mightiest monsters. Krakens, either alone or as a team of beasts, have been featured in many games, such as the role-playing game *Dungeons & Dragons* and computer games like *Total Annihilation: Kingdoms* and *Age of Mythology*. In the *Warhammer 40,000* universe, Kraken is an invading fleet, while in the game *Final Fantasy*, Kraken is a tentacled brute of the sea. Krakenlike characters appear often as boss monsters or boss enemies in the games, such as *Final Fantasy IX*, *Fable*, *Golden Sun*, *Dynamite Cop*, *Blaze and Blade*, *Shining Force II*, and *Ocean Hunter*. In *EarthBound*, the Kraken is a green sea serpent that provokes the hero. Tech Kraken, the Terror from the Deep in *Mega Man Zero 4s*, seeks revenge for his former master. Volt Kraken in *Mega Man X5* appears as a two-footed robot with arms like a human and a head with fins like a squid.

More **untraditional** kraken characters are featured in *Wonder Boy in Monster Land*, a Sega game, and in *Azure Dreams*, a PlayStation/Game Boy video game. In the first game, the creature is a boss monster that hovers over the ocean and shoots fireballs.

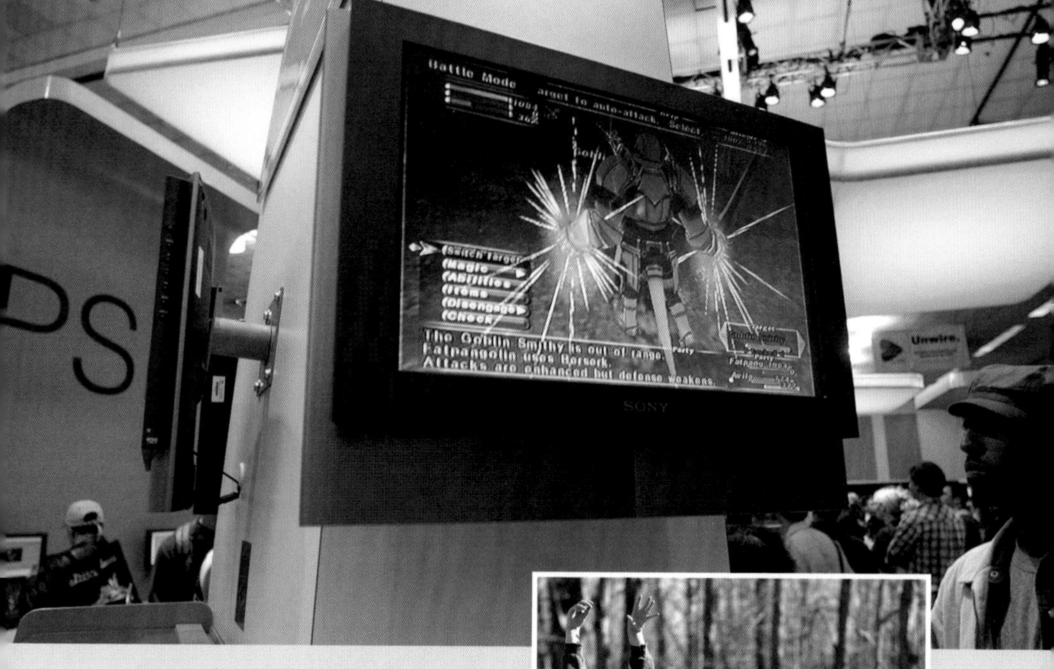

Two boys play the board game Dungeons & Dragons *in a park (right). Krakens appear in many games, including the role-playing game* Dungeons & Dragons. *The term "kraken" is used as a weapon, not as a character, in the PlayStation 2 game,* Final Fantasy XI *(above).*

In *Azure Dreams*, the Kraken does not dwell underwater. It floats and can electrocute other characters and nearby monsters. Tidal Kraken in the collectible card game *Magic: The Gathering* portrays a two-footed, four-armed sea beast that eats mermaids and pirates. The term "kraken" is also used for things other than a character. The Kraken Club is the most sought after weapon in the PlayStation 2 and PC game *Final Fantasy XI.* The club can attack up to eight times as if it has multiple

arms. In the online computer role-playing game, *Puzzle Pirates*, Kraken's blood is a dye.

A traditional kraken shows up in *Pirates of the Caribbean: Dead Man's Chest*, a PlayStation portable game by Sony. The monster is the final challenge. Players take on the role of Jack Sparrow and fight various enemies using speed and strength, as well as swords, pistols, throwing knives, and grenades. The beast's tentacles cause great damage to ships and humans, but players can injure it with cannon fire or explosions of powder kegs. When they defeat the Kraken, they win the game.

The famous sea creature has even invaded the music world and amusement parks. A band in Colombia, South America, goes by the name Kraken. The monster has been the theme of songs and has been featured on album covers and on shirts sold by bands on tour. At Sea World in Orlando, Florida, people hop aboard the Kraken, a bottomless roller coaster. Riders' feet dangle freely as the ride takes them fifteen stories high. The mechanical beast turns upside down seven times and travels 65 miles per hour (105km per hour).

In ancient times, the mysterious Kraken struck terror in the hearts of seafarers. Today the creature is known as the giant squid, and humans who encounter the animal are still filled with fright and amazement. No matter what it is called, the legendary monster continues to be one of the largest and most feared sea creatures ever.

Chapter 1: Legendary Sea Monster

1. Quoted in Richard Ellis, *The Search for the Giant Squid: The Biology and Mythology of the World's Most Elusive Sea Creature.* New York: Penguin Publishing, 1999, pp. 15–16.

Chapter 3: Forever Famous

2. Alfred Tennyson, *The Kraken, Alfred Lord Tennyson's Poetry, Collected Works.* http://home.att.net/~tennysonpoetry/ci.htm. Originally published: Alfred Tennyson, *The Kraken. POEMS, Chiefly Lyrical.* London: Effingham Wilson, Royal Exchange, Cornhill, 1830.

Glossary

Cape of Good Hope: A peninsula on the Atlantic coast of South Africa.

DNA: The main part of chromosomes; the material that transfers genetic characteristics in all life forms.

Falkland Islands: Islands in the South Atlantic Ocean, east of southern Argentina.

fathoms: Units of length equal to 6 feet (1.8m), used chiefly in oceanic measurements.

gargantuan: Gigantic; enormous; colossal.

habitat: The natural environment of an organism.

hallucination: A false image or impression; fantasy.

optical illusion: An observation of an image that is different from the way it really is.

phenomenon: A remarkable or unusual occurrence or circumstance.

plumbed: Measuring the depth of water or a hole by letting down a lead weight at the end of a line.

shape shift: Change appearance from one form to another.

specimen: A sample of a substance or material for examination or study.

undulate: Move in a wavelike motion.

untraditional: Unusual; not customary; not established.

For Further Exploration

Books

Eulalia Garcia, *Giant Squid: Monsters of the Deep*, Secrets of the Animal World. Milwaukee, WI: Gareth Stevens, 1997. This colorful volume describes the physical traits, habitat, behavior, and life cycle of these massive sea animals.

Bradford Matsen, *The Incredible Hunt for the Giant Squid*, Incredible Deep-Sea Adventures. Berkeley Heights, NJ: Enslow, 2003. This interesting book reveals what is known about the giant squid and the methods scientists use to learn more about the species.

Noel Peattie, *Hydra and Kraken, or, the Lore and Lure of Lake-Monsters and Sea-Serpents.* Oakland, CA: Regent Press, 1996. The stories in this book are taken from old records of frightening encounters with sea beasts.

Shirley Raye Redmond, *Tentacles! Tales of the Giant Squid.* New York: Random House, 2003. This fun book provides fascinating facts about the mysterious sea creature.

Internet Sources

Roger Hanlon, "Squid," NationalGeographic.com, August 2004, (http://magma.nationalgeographic.com/ngm/0408/feature2/index.html?fs=www3.nationalgeographic.com&fs=plasma.nationalgeographic.com). This article has wonderful photographs that show how fast giant squid can change their appearance.

Blake de Pastino, "Giant Squid Captured, Filmed for First Time," NationalGeographic.com, December 2006, (http://news.nationalgeographic.com/news/2006/12/061222-giant-squid.html). This exciting article shows the first photos ever taken of a live giant squid in the wild and the techniques used to lure the animal.

Web Sites

Dave's Mythical Creatures and Places (www.eaudrey.com/myth). This site covers a variety of make-believe beings, including the Devil Whale, Kraken, Nereid, Mermaid, Scylla, Siren, Sea Bishop, Sea Monk, Sea Horse, Sea Lion, Sea Serpent, and others.

In Search of Giant Squid (http://seawifs.gsfc.nasa.gov/squid.html). This center is sponsored by the Smithsonian Natural History Museum. It has a wide range of information about giant squid and compares them to other sea creatures.

Search for Giant Squid (www.mnh.si.edu/natural_partners/squid4). This center documents myths and facts concerning the giant squid and gives information about an expedition that searched for the haunts of this mysterious cephalopod.

INDEX

47

Picture Credits

Cover: © Bettmann/Corbis
AP Images, 14, 37, 37
© Bettmann/Corbis, 29
Carl De Souza/AFP/Getty Images, 24–25
© Corbis, 8
Hulton Archive/Getty Images, 19
Joanne Schmaltz/Photonica/Getty Images, 11
The Kobal Collection, 30
© National Science Museum/HO/epa/Corbis, 23
© Roger Tidman/Corbis, 15
© Stefano Bianchetti/Corbis, 21
© Underwood & Underwood/Corbis, 6–7
Walt Disney/The Kobal Collection, 32, 34–35

Jennifer Guess McKerley enjoys writing fiction and nonfiction for all ages. Her other nonfiction books for children include *Man o' War, Best Racehorse Ever, Amazing Armadillos*, and *Goblins*. She loves living in New Mexico. You can visit her Web site at www.jenniferguessmckerley.com.